melancholia

a collection of whispers

written by
LiAna Maria Rivera

*Dedicated to the lonely,
the grieving, and the brokenhearted.*

m e l a n c h o l i a

a journey awaits you in this book of rhymes.

a journey of sadness, weakness, despair, and heartbreak of all kinds.

the melancholia exists inside us all.

the melancholia is the fog in your mind, the dizziness before the fall.

the melancholia calls us by name.

a far cry from Heaven and Hell just the same.

the melancholia is isolation, depression, loneliness, grief. the absence of feeling yet tears still slide down your cheeks.

once you've entered the melancholia, there is no escape. the darkness will whisper sweet nothings against the skin of your nape.

the murky waters will wash your mask away, it will expose you in ways you never thought possible. it will strip you to your bare bones, ensnare you in its wrath. it will torture you relentlessly, but you won't feel a thing.

it will bring you to the brink of your own demise, and you must make the choice to live or to die.

this book of rhymes entails my journey through the melancholia.

you have been forewarned.

- d e n i a l -

melancholia

y o u n g . l o v e

I caught myself thinking about you again.
I try hard, but I never can forget.
The memories just linger endlessly in my mind.
All those times when you were so kind.
Once at the dance when you placed a kiss above my lip.
And the other time when I let everything slip.
I abandoned the fear that kept me sane
That cloudy April day when you kissed me in the rain.
I gave in to you and released my heart,
Thinking you'd never tear it apart.
Our embraces, our kisses,
They were all just figments.
For too many wasted years of my life,
I loved unconditionally.
But you, you hid everything.
You never, never truly loved me.
So, could young love ever be true?
Yes, yes, it was for me.
But never for you.

melancholia

melancholia

y e a r b o o k

You never finished writing that letter
inside the cover.
Most times I feel I should burn it
To erase our life from existence,
But the memories will remain
In every glossy, colorful page.
Pep rallies, clubs, and football games.
All our broken dreams immortalized
Inside an old, dusty book.
No matter how much I truly want to be
rid of it,
I know deep down, deep down, deep down,
This was the happiest time in my life.
And I cannot let it go, just yet.

melancholia

melancholia

o u r . 4 t h . o f . J u l y

Just a few years from today
Happy in the grass we laid.
Planning our own getaway
Oh, with you, I wish I stayed.

Hiding behind all the cars,
Your kisses left such happy scars
While you held me in your arms.
Though we never saw the stars.

Together we were invincible.
Our love was inconceivable.
To others we appeared so blind,
But our hearts were with our minds.

So, to you I dearly regret
That could not be with you yet.
As we were when we were young
Your name hung upon my tongue.

We're apart, but not completely.
Your essence will always be here with me.
In part of my heart, your soul shall stay,
Because you were
My soulmate.

melancholia

s o f t . g r e y . j a c k e t

This soft grey jacket kept me warm in the wind.
This soft grey jacket protected me through the night.
This soft grey jacket helped me find your light.
Your soft grey jacket clutched tightly in my hands.
Kept hope alive that I would see you again.

This soft grey jacket held me close when you left.
This soft grey jacket caught every tear that slid.
Your soft grey jacket shielded me from the fights.
And pulled the wool completely over my eyes.

A soft grey jacket passes through my mind.
Sitting in a pile of things you left behind.
The soft grey jacket never leaves my eye,
Visions of a soft grey jacket make me colder at night.
Coated with makeup and lingering tears,

melancholia

Your soft grey jacket clutched tightly in my hands
Reminds me every day, I'll never see you again.

melancholia

melancholia

p r o m i s e . r i n g

Remember when you gave me that
promise ring?
And told me you wanted to marry me?
Remember when I wore it every single
day,
Even after the silver wore away?

I held on tightly to your promise ring
It almost turned my entire thumb green
A size too big, you bought for me
So, I adorned it upon a necklace you gave
to me.

I buried all your old things.
Everything except that promise ring.
I kept it hidden from everyone
In a special place;
You needn't worry about your money
going to waste.

It will be forever by my heart
We will never truly be apart.
I'll keep it safely tucked away
And with me, our promise ring will never
stray.
As you did that fateful day.

melancholia

little.square.picture

We took selfies under the clouds
Whispered sweet nothings under
screaming crowds.
You held my hand and said this would last
forever.
So, I kissed you with the biggest smile on
my lips
And you snapped that Polaroid picture.
My hand on your neck and our eyes
fluttered shut
With our promise ring wrapped around
my thumb.
I wished it could have lasted forever,
Of course, it's still happening now
Inside that little square picture.
If I gaze at it for a moment, I feel a
lingering vacancy
Where your heartstrings used to be.
But when I stare at it for a while longer,
I can almost feel your breath against my
neck.
The tickling tingle left upon my lips,
And the softest blush I'd always get.
I am transported back to the time.
When I can pull your hair and touch your
cheek
And feel your heartbeat against mine.

melancholia

I can lay next to you and gaze up at the sky.
I can bask in a memory of broken sunlight.
Immortalized, our love had become.
Even after all was said and all was done.
But this is how I'll choose to remember it forever.
Every time I see that little square picture.

melancholia

h e a r t — s h a p e d . n o t e p a d

I wrote your name in a heart-shaped
notepad
And pressed it gently upon a love letter.
I sealed the envelope shut with a cherry
sweet kiss,
But I never sent it.
I wrote your birthday on a heart-shaped
notepad,
And placed it on my calendar, so I'd never
forget.
I wrote our anniversary on a heart-shaped
notepad
And hung it upon a wall inside my room.
So, I could always remember what it felt
like
To be in love with you.
I wrote your star sign on a heart-shaped
notepad,
Pressed it on my window, so you could
find me again.
Just like you always said.
When the day came
And I had nothing to say,
I stared at myself in the mirror.
My eyes bloodshot; tired from tears.
Dark makeup staining my cheeks in lines
of blue

melancholia

I drew a crack on my heart-shaped notepad,
And placed it over a picture of you.

melancholia

melancholia

h e . d i e d . a t . w a r

The man I love, he died at war,
A war against himself.
He ran away, he ran from me—
The one he asked for help.
To end the war inside his mind;
To heal his aching heart.
His love, the purest love—so strong!
Until it fell apart.
The man I love, he died at war.
A war against himself.
Let little demons poison his thoughts
To heal his aching heart.
And he fled from me, he hid from me,
From my breaking heart.
The man I love, he died at war.
A war against himself.
He lost the battle, let the darkness in.
After the long and woeful defeat,
A beautiful deception made me believe
The man I loved was back home with me.
My love for him grew stronger than ever
before.
But the man I loved,
The man I loved
Was lost, forevermore.

melancholia

g r i e f

I grieve for the one I love, someone who loved me
And you ask, "Why do you still have his stuff?
"Throw it away!
"He was never good for you anyway."
Yes, yes, you're right, but only who he became.
Not the one who gave me his heart—
Someone who loved me.
And you say, "Why do you still keep his things?"
I grieve for the one I love, the one who loved me.
I keep his old clothes and cheap jewelry,
A worn hoodie, his letters, an emerald ring.
A song he wrote for me.
A video game he bought me.
Old earbuds he lent me.
Stuffed animals he gave me.
The promises he made me.
I grieve for the one I love—someone who loved me.
That man is dead,
Torn away by reality.
Good things never last, not really.

melancholia

If you ask me again, "Why do you keep his things?"
Know that I am only grieving
For someone who once loved me.
The chapters in that book
Will linger forever in loving memory.
I always knew he'd eventually die,
It was simply a matter of time.
We'll both meet new people down the line,
But who he once was—
The one who loved me;
That one will always be mine.

melancholia

melancholia

d a n c i n g

We went to a dance that spring in high school.
I remember it like it was yesterday.
Your eyes were bright
The youngest night,
All worries seemed to fade away.
Around that time, you didn't know
That I was supposed to go.
Now I'm here, my first year in college
Attending my first dance since then.
And I could have sworn I saw you dancing tonight.
With your arms wrapped around someone tight.
But it did not bother me even the slightest bit.
Because I knew that you were not him.
Remember when I refused to dance with you,
That beautiful night in high school?
I'm ever so grateful I understood even then.
Because, don't you see?
Don't you see?
Only a foolish girl could truly believe,
That you would ever come back to me.

melancholia

melancholia

s l a s h e s . a n d . d a s h e s

I still remember the first text you sent.
It was a picture of a cat
Made of slashes and dashes.
So, I laughed and smiled.
Such a naïve child…

I remember the first text you sent.
After I said "Yes."
It was a picture of a heart.
No slashes or dashes,
What a wonderful start!

And I remember the last text you sent.
It has been the hardest to forget.
Even after I had read it over and over in my head,
I couldn't shake away the emptiness.
So, I sent you a text.
A picture of a heart—and in the middle
… a slash.

melancholia

d a i l y . r o u t i n e

Hello, my love. It is three o'clock pm.
My cell phone lights up; an old picture—
forgotten.
I resist the strongest urge to answer
Placing it gently upon the counter.
I walk to my room and lock myself inside.
As I feel the burns of that scorching
summer light,
Filtering through my windows as the sun
fades from my life.
The same pain I felt when you left me
behind.
I squeeze my eyes shut, but it does not
end.
Leftover wounds—too late to mend.
The tears I thought had run dry.
Tears I was never able to cry.
Spill from my eyes like frosted ice
Melting rapidly in sunlight.
With nothing else left to do, I begin to
write.
The pain, just write, write, write it away!
Into something beautiful, these feelings
may change.
I gather my bearings after writing a few
more lines.
And convince myself that I am in a clear
state of mind.

melancholia

Until I hear our song playing in my head.
So, I lay down and weep to myself on my bed.
I had already taken a shower that morning,
Yet I desperately feel the need to do it again.
I rush past the phone as it lights up with your face once more.
Then isolate myself in the bath,
Like I have so many times before.
Against my burning skin, this water is freezing cold
And I shiver in drizzling sprinkles and do not dare move,
Because I know that once I do, once I do,
I'll more than likely be tempted by you.
I wait until the last possible second to switch the water warm.
And take precious time washing up.
I am done cleansing sooner than desired,
So, I stand in the tub far longer than required.
From a thin mist of steam and fog,
I finally emerge and pass by the blinking light.
This time I click it on to check the time.

Now, my love, it is five.

melancholia

Three missed calls and one voicemail from you,
The one who ruined my life.
I resist unlocking the phone,
Throwing it across the sofa in my living room.
Then I get dressed.
After I take the longest time possible to be ready:
Changing my outfit in a row of three,
Drying, straightening, curling my hair,
Layer after layer of a full face—
Wearing as much makeup as I could take.
Finally, I'm able to make
A healthy meal for my own sake.
I eat it slowly, in no rush at all.
And finally, finally, finally, I do not hear your call.
After dinner, I wipe my face,
Until there is none left—a trace.
Then I turn on the TV to see the time.

It is twelve o'clock midnight.
I do not yet feel tired though,
So, I re-watch an episode of my favorite show.
Three times in a row.
When I feel groggy, I see the time,
To realize it struck four o'clock at night.

melancholia

I walk into my room and stay locked up inside.
Forcing myself to close my eyes.
And when I wake up, I check the time.

Red light contrasts with the darkness in my room.
The time now reads twelve o'clock noon.
Yawn, stretch, and get ready.
Wash up, cook breakfast, and turn on the tele.
Afterwards, with nothing else left,
I pick up my phone.
It is dead.
I shrug and think nothing of it.
And into the charger, I plug it.
Then I sit and jot down ideas that bounce in my head.
When I decide to look at my phone again,

Two hours have passed; it is two o'clock pm.
I see the calls and listen to the voicemail.
It is you on the phone, once again.
Your voice pierces my heart, it digs deeper and deeper.
Just before I lose control,
Now I know what I've always known…
These feelings linger much too deep,
It will never matter how much I sleep.

melancholia

What we once were is trapped inside my head.
And I will never, ever, ever be sane again.

"Hello, my love. It is three o'clock pm."

melancholia

t h e . a c h i n g . r i n g

Can you hear it?
The ring on the other end?
The dial tone?
No answer.
Call again.
Voicemail.
Hearing his voice on the other side:
"Leave a message so I can call you back."
But will he?
No.
Tears overflowing.
"Are you crazy?"
No, I'm not crazy.
"You're in denial.
It's over, it's done.
Stop calling."
The aching ring.
I can't stop.
The aching ring.
The tone on the other end.
Hope?
"No."
Hope is lost.
"You're crazy!"
No, I'm not crazy.
Can you hear it?
The aching ring.
It's loud in my ear.

melancholia

You can't hear it?
"No."
The sound of his voice.
The aching ring.
The aching ring.
The echo in my head.
"Where's the phone?"
It's in my head.
The aching ring.
The aching ring.
"He'll never answer."
Yes, he will.
He will, he will!
The aching ring.
The aching ring.
Filling my ears.
Filling my eyes.
The aching ring.
"Please don't cry."
The aching ring.
The aching ring.
The tears… drip, drop,
Dripping, dropping?
The aching ring.
The aching ring.
Just come clean.
The aching ring.
The aching ring.
You don't love me?
The aching ring,

melancholia

The aching ring.
Stop calling,
Please stop calling.
The aching ring,
The aching ring,
The aching ring…

melancholia

melancholia

c o n f l i c t e d

They all said I'd move on with time,
But it feels like I'm living in a nightmare
without you
I'm still stuck remembering a happier
yesterday;
So please just leave me alone,
But please don't go.

- guilt -

melancholia

v i r g i n . h e a r t

An untouched heart is one of great
fragility:
Feathery, light, airy skips.
Rhythms regular; a song through my lips!
Before he weakened my purity
With each pulse quickening,
And a sound so sickening
Of hissing whispers.
His sweet words bled into my virgin ears;
I ever so foolishly let him
Litter his kisses across my body.
It felt so right, and so guilty.
All feelings within contradicted me!
Until my virgin heart was in his grasp,
He kept breathing lies into my mind—
Clutching tightly in a pleasure sublime,
And I was worthless in my endeavor,
'Twas my heartstrings he severed…

melancholia

melancholia

h e a v e n

You and I, we made it together.
Despite our blackened, tainted feathers.
A special place where we would hide,
The place where happiness resides.
I want so desperately to be
In that utopia, forever free.
A paradise; a wonderful place—
Where our newfound love was filled with grace.
That world of brisk air, and your gentle kiss
Because in my heart, it still exists.
So, to this life, I'll say goodbye.
And wait for you on the other side.
Maybe soon you'll realize.
Heaven is never very far,
For those who bear such heavy scars.

melancholia

melancholia

h o m e l e s s

Without him, she's homeless.
His eyes, his hair, his face—
The breeze, the kisses, the smell of the
freezing sea;
The trees, the trails, the hill,
Another life where they were free.
Being with him was the only place
She felt like she belonged,
But she's no longer welcome there
In a place that was once her home.
So now, love, riddle me this:
Without you, I'm homeless
So where am I to go?

melancholia

melancholia

t h e . t r u t h

Even now, we both know the truth.
The one you keep hidden, even from you.
But you cannot escape it, can you?
It's buried deep inside your head.
One of the darkest fantasies you ponder
While you lie awake in bed.
With your cold, white fingers coated with frosted tips,
And when the taste of her name still lingers on your lips.
Truth is, this will never end
Because you will never have her back again.

melancholia

melancholia

b e l o n g

Where do I belong when I'm not with you?
Whose am I if not yours?
I'm stuck here at a loss,
Because I shall never know the cause.
Of why you left.
What had I done
That was so unforgivable to you?
What had I done
To trigger this?
These unanswered questions leave me restless.
Pointless wonders that trail throughout my mind.
Every waking moment of every living day.
I don't know why I keep asking, but
Where do I belong when I'm not with you?
You will never tell the truth.

melancholia

melancholia

t h o u g h t s

You sense it, don't you?
The darkness looming over your head,
Every moment you hear of her?
The heaviness inside your chest—
You feel it inside,
And you think about it all the time,
And it always lingers in the back of your mind.
That one day, one day, someday soon—
You know 'tis true, 'tis true, 'tis true—
She will find someone better than you.

melancholia

melancholia

b l i n d

A body of light; the sun bounces off his
skin.
Orbs of blue, disappear beneath deep
waters.
With a kiss, he pulls the soul from my lips
And frozen hands barely touch my skin;
Stealing my vessel of its purity.
Fresh breaths of his air spread
Like a plague into my lungs
As my eyes slide shut in ecstasy,
Unknown sensations pulse inside of me
Before I forget to breathe.
His soft lashes kiss my lids
And when I lift them to gaze back at him,
All I can see
… is darkness.

melancholia

melancholia

d r o w n i n g

One day, I fear I may drown in the sea.
Will that be the end?
Until I choke in the sliver
Surround me in rain—the egregious river.
Flooding deeply into my lungs,
But the taste of him still lingers upon my tongue!
It will take time before I could breathe again.
Because I miss his eyes so much,
I can drown in them.

melancholia

melancholia

f r o s t b i t e

His frost-bitten hands cradled her heart.
Icicle eyes—
Glazed over in white.
The sound of the snow sang her to sleep.
The wind carried his voice through the air.
Before she breathed in a careful kiss,
And choked on frozen tears.

melancholia

melancholia

e y e . o f . a q u a r i u s

Dead of winter
January twenty-second.
Bitter cold breaths
Against my white dress
Soft mists kiss my skin
In my airy decent.
The sun reflects prisms—colors
Cascading in a shining sheet of satin
As I bask in a whirling wind.
An unknown force beckons me.
Frozen fingers grasp my neck,
Cold lips against my ear.
An enchanting song through my voice
whispers softly:

"… Eye of Aquarius."

melancholia

s t a t i c

Our love was like static
Messy and scattered.
Your kiss reminds me of the sunset
breeze.
Your eyes black and grainy in my head,
The memories play over again and again.

Pause and rewind this VCR tape
Of our old life
A sacrifice so vain.
Our love was like snow on a TV screen,
I welcomed the toxins that burned so deep
Like a vintage video tape from 1930.
You entered my mind through my mouth,
my eyes.
Imprints and scars and wounds left
behind.
The blood spilt over my lips, my teeth;
Skin bared, tired, naked and weak.

Our love was like static
Messy and scattered.
Although it was toxic,
You were all that mattered.
Of such aching numbness, I'll never be
free
Because our love was static on a TV
screen.

melancholia

The blizzard's loud and angry;
Broken and bleak.

melancholia

melancholia

s k i d . m a r k

He left a mark on my heart—
A black aged tire trail like a tattoo
Sinking deeper than the surface.
I can cover it up,
But I know it's still there.
Yes, I can surely pretend
That it doesn't exist.
But inside, I can feel it;
The skid mark still beats against my chest.
And weakens every haunting breath.

melancholia

melancholia

t u r n t a b l e . o f . m e m o r i e s

He keeps finding his way back into my mind.
Like a record on a turntable spinning away.
'Round and 'round, it goes.
The memory of him makes me dizzy
I cannot be free!
There still lingers inspiration.
I hear the sounds play on that old record album.
His voice resounds throughout my room.
It echoes into the vacant halls.
This turntable plays songs that were ours
A tune familiar and strong
And fragile and shattered.
The memories of him play on my turntable,
And with every sound—
'Round and 'round
The dizziness kisses my head through the clouds
Seeing the album spin
'Round and 'round;
And in that aching, gut-wrenching sound,
I drown… I drown.

melancholia

melancholia

s o u l l e s s

Caress my soft, soft, soft skin,
Comb my woven hair with skinny
fingers—cold as ice.
Paint my lips red with a salt-sweet kiss,
And rest your freezing hand upon my hip.
Dress me up in lace and satin,
And dance, dance, dance with me into
oblivion…

Bury me away in your old box of
memories—
Let my big brown eyes haunt you while
you sleep.
Something brewing within my chest hath
cracked.
And despite a lively deceiving mask,
You no longer hold
My soul in your grasp.

melancholia

melancholia

s t u n g

Warm, cozy, silly love
Chapped and sticky kisses
His beard was barely a tickle
With curly cues upon his chin.
Little nippy bites pricked my neck
And an icy cold lick against my lips.
His love was sweet—addicting;
Honey from a wild bumblebee
A serum so sweet, in fact that I
Let him sting me every time.
The kisses released toxins into my veins
That cost me my sanity.
Fuzzy numbness pricked at my heart
Buzzing pain; everlasting.

melancholia

melancholia

m a s k

I told him I covered myself with a mask.
Removing it, for him, was a simple task.
This mask shielded me from feeling the pain.
But now it's seeping back again.
His cold skinny fingers traced my skin,
Through the holes of my eyes,
And the sides of my face,
My hazy façade has been erased.
It falls, it falls, into the abyss.
Of everlasting emptiness.

- anger -

melancholia

b u r d e n

All the things I've written so far,
Only serve this book as small stones unturned.
I cannot put it into words,
Everything you have done that has made me hurt.
And that burden is one that I must carry,
Because I know deep down
You'll never understand the agony
Of everything I've felt since that fateful summer day
When you left me alone to deal with the pain.

Warm stones and pebbles of what used to be us
Are now lost in an endless river of teardrops
And that burden is one that you must carry,
Knowing that everything you have done,
Is the core of what truly ruined us.

melancholia

melancholia

f a t h e r ' s . d a y

This would have been a letter for Father's Day,
But it seems my father has gone away.
Fondly I look upon the times when I was a child,
Though I know he's felt this way for a while.
And now it seems my mother has grown quite tired.
For all our time in his life has expired.
Our broken family had never been so whole,
Before he decided to walk out the door.
This could have been a letter for Father's Day.
But I believe my father has ran away.
He abandoned the love of his few children,
To live a lustful life filled with ruin.
I cannot speak for the eldest ones,
But I know his time—for me, is done.
This should have been a letter for Father's Day,
Instead my cowardly father chose to run away.

melancholia

a.c a s t l e . i n . c r u m b l e s

He took the waves and beach away
Isolated us inside a cold empty castle.
Rainbows, mountains, and waterfalls
All child dreams of mine lie in crumbles.
We left footprints in the sand,
My family and him;
His previous life with us—crushed in rubble.
I lived in many a castle when I was young
Where I danced to show tunes and silly songs.
A turntable spun as I twirled across the floor.
Naïve in my stride
Filled with hope and dreams, my bright eyes gleamed.
Though all I have achieved was not enough.
Our families' castle found home in rubble.
Constructed from the pride of a guilty man,
Now lies vacant in a state of ruin
Filled with boxes of photographs and picture books;
Family moments captured on old VCR tapes;
Everything has now, turned moldy and gray.

melancholia

Every single memory—burned away
I have changed my maiden name.
I fled from that plain-walled castle
Drenched in his deceit.
I refuse to let my family crumble
And left him behind in all the rubble.

melancholia

melancholia

l o c k s . a n d . k e y s

Shlock, Creak,
Shriek, Click!
Keep her safe, use a lock and a key.
Keep her safe from him,
From me.
Keep her safe from even thee
And seal her shut with a lock and a key.
Shlock, Creak,
Shriek, Click!
A metal framework cages her—
The element of eeriest benevolence.
A key with ragged edges seals it shut;
'Tis impossible to pick it free.
Keep her under a lock
And a key
Of the vaguest intricacy.
Shlock, Creak,
Shriek, Click!
I cast the bronze key into the flames
To ensure I'll never go insane.
I watch the key melt in the heat
Finally, I feel at ease.
Keep this heart sealed under a lock and a melted key.
For he will never again break me.

- d e p r e s s i o n -

melancholia

d e p r e s s i o n

I could not save him from it like he saved
me. I could not free him like he freed me.
Depression is such a cruel disease.
It lingers in the back of your mind,
Almost impossible to find.
In your head, it is always present;
And once it takes hold,
It will never let go.
It will never leave you, and it's quite
unpleasant.
Depression is like this analogy.
So, imagine and listen well, listen well to
me.

You're stuck in traffic.
You're frustrated.
You just want to go,
You want to go home.
And finally, the line moves; it's clear,
you're free.
Every little part of you beams with glee.
Foolish as you are, you make it a game.
Race against the green light—
Nothing stands in your way.
You're almost there, you're almost home.
Colors bleed together and clash
Too fast to think; too soon to react,
Just go!

melancholia

You can make it, you're almost home!
But you fail to look both ways.

So, you crash.

Headlights shatter as you freeze in fear.
A tank of gas is punctured in the havoc.
Putrid liquid leaks onto you—
Engulfed in a fiery panic.
It burns through every inch of the space,
Until your skin flickers and lights up in
flames.
The heat spreads further as you lay still.
When suddenly, your eyes snap open to
see
Thin, scorched flesh sweeping across your
body
Shaking in fright!
Cling desperately to life; because in that
moment,
You want to survive.
But it is too late, and you cannot wait.
With no strength left in you, all you can
do is scream;
And pray it's all just a terrible dream.
You cry for someone to come through the
fiery encasement that boils your veins.
To cleanse your body that aches with
pain.

melancholia

You struggle in a fight alone to take
breath after breath,
And you die a hindered and agonizing
death.

My biggest regret, you may ask?
The love of my life;
A casualty of strife.
I finally found him,
But missed the signs.
His face ashen, pale;
His lips blistered wine.
I could not free him from the fire;
I was too late.
I never should have made him wait.
Because when the flames finally burnt out,
He was nowhere to be found.
The love of my life, he was lost.
Now I'm the one who must pay the cost.

Depression burned away the love from his
soul,
And now, never will I ever completely be
whole.
Depression was the sinister culprit of this
theft.
And now depression is all that is left.

The darkness is back; it replaces the light.
The darkness is back; I have lost the fight.

melancholia

p r o m i s e

You'll always be there, that's what you
Promised me,
During a time when you loved
Unconditionally.
Such a lovely lie that turned out to be.
I thought you spoke to me truthfully.
But somehow, somehow you trapped me,
In an infinite loop of despondency.

melancholia

melancholia

g r a y

Bright sun beaming across my face
With every touch of his embrace.
Everything 'round is gleaming with color
Until I feel crackling thunder.
Clouds roll in and cloak the sky,
We're trapped alone without a light.
He pulls away,
Fades to gray,
Stares at me with such a scary sight,
And whispers to me softly, "Goodnight."

melancholia

melancholia

f o g . a n d . h a z e

A weeping cloud hovers over me.
And I can't feel anything.
I can only see his face.

Translucent drops freeze me—inside out.
Fog and rain is a cold mist,
Where goosebumps bloom
Across my skin.

He is always on my mind.
Though now it seems our fates
Shall never again intertwine.
Yet here I remain
In a permanent state

Of fog and haze.

melancholia

melancholia

m o n o c h r o m e . h e a r t

I lived in a world of black and white
When he lifted me into the sky.
With a kiss from his lips, I tasted the sea.
This heart, before—grey and bleak
Was drowned inside a roaring ravine
Of pink and red and rapid beats.
This world of mine was bathed in light,
No shadows to taunt me in the night.
Eventually though, I fell through the cracks
He did not try to save me from its wrath.
It started with my eyes, it did.
The cold spread throughout my fingertips.
Until the rest of my body became
Monochrome grey.
There was no time left for me.

The tragic story ended there,
A wasteland of oak and leaves
This tragic story of love lost
Shall never again know peace.

melancholia

b l a c k . a n d . w h i t e

I was black.
He was white.
He left behind too many scars
In the shape of a bleeding heart.
When I shut off my mind
And close my eyes,
I feel his lips against mine;
Before I am awakened in a malevolent
dream!
He was black
And I was white.
He burned high up into the sky
I froze like snowflakes in airy moonlight.
I held on to our heart of grey
And melded it into my own.
Since then both hearts no longer beat
With air and blood like rushing streams.
Instead they lie still, broken, and battered.
Old from age,
Dry from drought,
And frozen from the inside out.

melancholia

melancholia

r o s e

I was once a rose.
A vision of soft petals amid bloom,
Radiant red;
Sharp thorns on my stem.
Until he pulled me from my roots,
Caressed my petals with cold as blue
hands,
And clipped my thorns away.
Then he placed me inside a glass vase
The color of his eyes,
And drowned me.
Slowly, but surely, I felt myself decay.
And when my petals turned a dull shade of
death,
And my leaves dried out,
He emptied me back into the ground,
But, you see within my home
There had been a drought.

melancholia

a m e t h y s t . g e m

In the basement, I found an amulet
With an amethyst gem in its center.
Atop and below—the ends were sharp;
Pricked my finger like thorns on roses.
Alone I found myself in a haze
Of nostalgia as I gazed
Into the glass that shielded the gem.
It distorted my vision across to the other side
In which I saw a mirrored reflection of me.
The band attached broke off easily
Like the thin string that tied us together.
But it was tied too tight,
Snapped off one side,
And the amulet fell soon after.
The glass hit the ground, and the gem was exposed.
A metaphorical performance of love that was gone.
Now I sit in my bed,
Soft like a cloud,
Springy and breaking and creaking and loud.
You had gone away into the light
And left me alone to stare into the night.
What was left in your wake; an amulet glowing?

melancholia

Memories and pictures projecting onto the walls!
From the hopeful beginning of such innocent love,
To the bitter end of our special song.

melancholia

w i l d f i r e

Love between us was a wildfire.
Sweet kisses broke purple bruises,
Careful caresses lit matches; butterflies
were gasoline!
It spread vast and wide yet drowned out
in a flash.
This love of ours, burned ever bright
Yet for you, the well ran dry.
Small embers and flickers touched the
grass
Littered with your drought,
Lighting our secret woodland ablaze.
All attempts to save me went in vain
When you spread your wings and flew
away,
Dropping me inside the blazing flames.
From the eye of the storm, I gazed
As our haven burned to bleak.
This vessel of mine shook in the heat
O such wrathful agony!
After a long while, the rain finally came
And bathed all remnants of our Hill in
grey.
I wandered inside our forest—destroyed.
Ashes left behind from dried petals of
roses.
In the time it took for the smoke to clear,
My voice was found in the river near.

melancholia

And through every scream and every sob
I sang a song of love and loss.

melancholia

t h e . p o n d

Falling in love for the first time—
It's like laying atop a pond of ice.
The warmth of your body melts the lake
Like his smile melts your sanity.
The outline of you and him above the depths
Becomes a nefarious silhouette.
Your heart shivers when foreign feelings arise,
From a man who fed you little lies.

Your eyes slide shut
Give to your newfound love
The irreplaceable gift of trust.
But evil lurks within all of us,
And the man you chose to love,
He had been the darkest one.

You lie on a pond of cracking ice
As the snow sinks the lake around you.
And inside you pray,
Believe he may
Come to your rescue.
But instead from within the depths,
He reaches for your neck.
His cold hand paralyzes your spine
As he pulls you inside a crack in the ice.

melancholia

For a long time,
You will fight
Beneath the pond of cracking ice
Until he claims your life.
But if you manage to save yourself,
Your soul shall be broken.
If you manage to save yourself,
Your heart shall be frozen.

melancholia

melancholia

a . b r o k e n . l o v e . s o . n u m b

He held her and said he wouldn't leave;
But he did.
She says she's all right
Yet, the memories are killing her;
Like the knife he left behind
Carving out each vein in her slow beating heart,
But only with him could she feel such things:
Pain, love, hate; and even–
Happiness?

"Kill me." she said,
"Because if you feel nothing,
You might as well be dead;
and without you, love… I am dead."

He pondered, considering her selfless plea,
Knowing if he did, then he would be free.
And so, he plunged the knife into her heart.
Wrapped in his grey hood of northern air,
Tears peeked beneath her lashes;
And she drifted off to eternal sleep.

melancholia

melancholia

s m a l l . t o w n

I moved to a small town
And fell in love with the color blue.
His eyes were light back then;
The same haunting hue of the sky
When our innocent dreams illuminated
the night.

I moved to a small town and fell in love
with that sky.
The clouds overhead the same color of his
skin; pale.
A translucent ghost is all that he is to me
now.
I moved to a small town and fell in love
with the sea.
That now surrounds an island of grief
Only accessible through bridge and boat.
I no longer feel the warmth in his coat.
I used to live in a small town tinted in
grey and blue;
But now all our memories have turned
grey too.

-acceptance-

melancholia

m o d e s t . l i f e

I would have been happy living with you.
But you never even let me choose.
I could have lived that modest life,
With no one, but you by my side.
And only now have I realized
That my life wasn't meant to be lived with you.
Both of us are happier now
Split in two.

melancholia

melancholia

l – o – v – e

Love is a word spelled L-O-V-E
It is not for you, or for me.
What is love? Asked by many.
It is a spell that forces us to our knees.
It makes it so that we cannot see.
All are trapped, all of we.
This "we" includes you and me.
Both of us were never free,
Because seldom is it ever meant to be.

melancholia

melancholia

f a d e

We were happy, laughing; full of life.
Until we both ran out of time.
We believed so strong, that we were alive,
It was only beginning then;
We didn't know back when,
You and I—
That we were slowly losing the fight.
Now, my love, it seems that I
Have simply faded into the night.

melancholia

melancholia

i m a g i n a r y

Clear, translucent, shining glass;
I can see a scene through a filtered lens.
A blur passing through warns me,
I don't acknowledge the feeling.
As it sinks deep inside my being.
A window smudged with a lipstick stain
Distorts the vision—a clear image of him.
See, I thought I saw him staring at me
through the glass
But alas, alas, alas, at last
His presence there had swiftly passed.

melancholia

melancholia

f o r g o t t e n

There was a time I didn't think it was possible.
To forget anything about you.
Of course, most memories linger on,
The scent of your jacket,
And the taste of your tongue,
And the sound of your voice is clear in my mind.
Even now I believe these memories will persist forever
Or until my brain goes rotten.
But your name it seems, to me at least,
Has already been forgotten.

melancholia

melancholia

c r o s s r o a d

I stood at a crossroad
Wondering who I should be.
The breaker, the killer, a reaper of dreams.
And inside I knew, in my head, it was right.
But instead, I left you to decide.
I chose the kind, easier way,
And slowly led my fragile heart to break.

I stood at a crossroad,
Gazed up at the signs.
A reason unbeknownst to me,
I did not heed their warning.
You told me to close my eyes,
And I did so; I never asked why.
You grabbed my hand, and led me astray
And I convinced myself that either way
I would be okay.

Now I stand at a crossroad
Wondering who I've become.
The broken, the wanderer, a ghost of the past,
And I finally see what has always been.
That you and I were never meant to last.

melancholia

melancholia

n o t h i n g . l e f t

I sit to write a countless number of pages.
Wracking my brain,
Trying to remember the good things,
But I've written them all down by now.
There is nothing left.

melancholia

melancholia

h e a r t . o f . g l a s s

Soft pulsations—
Rushing, pumping, breathing
Breaking.
Punctured beats; a shard of glass
When the theoretical organ had fallen
from his grasp.
Shattered in pieces—
Uneven alignments.
I am left to pick up the fragments
And construct one anew that is of great
fragility.
Now this transparent heart of glass
… shall be my legacy.

About the Author:

LiAna Maria Rivera is an artist of various mediums namely: writing, drawing, and music.

Her purpose in life is to call the inner melancholy that lay dormant within her and transform it into something beautiful in any creative way her mind wills it.

Her writing and art styles are heavily inspired by the romantic era of art and literature. As expected, she loves writing poetry, horror, and psychological thrillers. Despite this, she's a softie for beautiful love stories and likes to incorporate themes of love into a vast majority of her work.

She loves animals, but no animal more than Mr. BooBooKitty Cuddles, a black and white seven year young cat. Rainy, cloudy days spent cuddling with him and getting lost in a book are what happy times are made of for this strange lady. When she's not cooing over how adorable her cat is, she's probably writing a blog post about how the decomposition process makes flowers shine brighter than the Supermoon.

For more information, visit her on Instagram @rosesintheriver !

melancholia: a collection of whispers
copyright © 2019 by LiAna Maria Rivera.
No part of this book may be used or
reproduced in any manner without
written permission except in the case of
reprints in the context of reviews.

ISBN: 978-1-951417-00-0

Library of Congress Control Number:
2019913223

Cover Design and Illustrations by LiAna
Maria Rivera

Read the story that inspired the poetry! melancholia: a graphic storytelling is available to read for free on Webtoon!

www.ingramcontent.com/pod-product-compliance
Lightning Source LLC
Chambersburg PA
CBHW030118100526
44591CB00009B/445